Learning to see in tl

for Mary —

Enjoy!

Lorraine Janzen

Sept 1st, 2003

Learning to see in the dark

Lorraine Janzen

Wolsak and Wynn . Toronto

Typeset in Garamond, printed in Canada by The Coach House Printing Company, Toronto.

Front cover art: © Shelley Wall
Cover design: The Coach House Printing Company
Author's photograph: David Brown Photography

The publisher gratefully acknowledges support from the Canada Council for the Arts and the Ontario Arts Council for their support through a block grant.

Wolsak and Wynn Publishers Ltd.
192 Spadina Avenue, Ste #315
Toronto, ON
Canada M5T 2C2

The Canada Council   Le Conseil des Arts
for the Arts   du Canada

ONTARIO ARTS COUNCIL
CONSEIL DES ARTS DE L'ONTARIO

National Library of Canadian Cataloguing in Publication

Janzen, Lorraine, 1953-
        Learning to see in the dark / Lorraine Janzen.

ISBN 0-919897-93-2

        I. Title.

PS8569.A5869L43 2003   C711',6   C2003-902370-2
PR9199.4.J65L43 2003

for John

Contents

Gravity and grace I   11
Discovery poems
    I   Tecumseh Street   12
    II   Indian dust   14
    III   Hawkeye   16
    IV   New world   18
    V   Indian summer   20
Psalms for great-grandfathers   21
Sunday best   24
Time out of mind   26
Always wear a slip, or things my mother taught me   30
Pie poems
    I   Flaky 1   33
    II   Pie in the sky   34
    III   Nightmare   36
    IV   Apple pie   37
    V   Rolling pin   38
    VI   Dough   40
    VII   Birth   43
    VIII   Flaky 2   44
Cross-dressing, or one is not born a woman   45
Alice poems
    I   Alison Wonderland   48
    II   White knight   50
    III   Alice underground   52
Graveyard tunes   53
Ghost   55
Preservings   57
Dead woman talking   59
Dead secret   61

Harbouring angels unawares   62
Singing the sacred   63
Wise woman's garden   65
Naming poem for a naming day   67
Martindale Pond   68
Winter rain   69
Seasonal cycle
    I   Winter Woman   71
    II   Spring Beauty   72
    III   Lady of Lakes   73
    IV   Autumn dancer   74
Champlain Island   75
Gravity and grace II   76

Acknowledgements   79

Gravity and grace I

for John

This is the shape of love, the heft and hew
of it, like a cat stretching in the sun,
longer than longing. Like a moon gone un
der water, shining and sure. Like a beau
tiful vein of quartz in granite, a view
of islands from a rocky shore, a run
over miles of pine-tree trails, to the one
place that knows you forever, that holds you
like bedrock. I've carved my initials here.
Now I'm building a monument of stone
upon stone upon stone. How can we know
gravity and grace unless we live near
the edge of cliffs – unless we cut to bone
our bare selves so spirit can come and go.

Discovery poems

1492-1992

I
Tecumseh Street

Walking down Tecumseh Street
schoolbag swinging
and feet drumming the beat
of the class recitation

> *Where I walk to school each day*
> *Indian children used to play*

I've got one foot on the sidewalk
and the other on a dirt trail,
dark woods moving in and out
between stucco bungalows,
canoes on the canal.

Shuffling the leaves of past and present
I see footsteps everywhere
shadows so deep
you could disappear forever:
hidden paths and imagined circles.

I walk like my father
feet wide, heels firm,
toes splayed out.
I have to force my feet in
to walk these unaccustomed steps,
redirect maybe 500 years
to match my stride
with these silent prints.

Tracking the road with another's grace,
listening to another chant,
as I look for ghosts on Tecumseh Street –

Look not for ghosts but for children playing
and calling me to join.

II
Indian dust

Opa bought the land on Niagara Street,
made a farm with his sons. The women hoeing,
planting, picking, sorting, packing. The men
driving tractor, spraying fruit,
loading baskets in the pickup for market.
Children playing all around.

I'd climb the silo to see the farm
spread out like a wheel –
Round rim of hills and creeks,
white roads spoking through orchards and fields.
At the centre, the familiar farmyard circle:
our house, packing shed, two houses
for uncles and aunts, tool shed, chicken coop, barn –
and up a little hill, Opa and Oma's house by the willow.

Circle of buildings and outlying land
my whole wheel of fortune then.
Family everywhere
living and working with each other.
Me with many parents loving and disregarding
Wandering through orchards eating peaches,
discarding clothes and dancing in the valley,
mounding up piles of Indian dust
on the farm road by our house
so I could watch the fine white cloud
rise and dissolve into blue air
when the flatbed trailer rolled through.

Wondering even then why we all called it *Indian dust*
and thinking now we found forgotten figures
in the sand, heard the land sing of other children
with many parents, other plantings and buildings;
lifting their voices on earth motes in the sun,
as she told her tale to the sky with the delicate dance
of her dusty children and then took them back
to her deep and careful keeping, her unending song –
a handful of sand sifting the sonorous years.

III
Hawkeye

Schoolroom in Port Weller. Hot afternoon
and rows full of kids I don't know
from the other side of the canal.
Dutch and English and German and Native,
blond and black heads bent over books.
Flies buzzing in windows angled at 45 degrees
or spinning in angry circles on the floor.

Outside behind the trees a boat travels
slowly up the canal, siren shriek telling me
there's another waiting in the lock.

         I sit and dream
of other times in this place
before concrete and print
before cold wars and fear huddled
with raised arms under desks;
straightening my spine and starting to write
at the sound of precise footsteps
clicking down the hall and pausing
by our door as Hawkeye examines
our silent backs, touching our work
with his fierce and sudden presence,
his upright carriage and erect head
with its bristling Mohawk cut.

Hawkeye
carrying cultural memory for all of us
with his stern unrelenting drive, his pride
in the plaids and economies of his Scottish father,
the wood lore and lineage of his Iroquois grandmother.
Teaching us to love this land and its histories,
offering Canada to us daily with the strength
of his body. Sharp eyes flinty with anger and hope.

IV
New world

We jump and jump, the waves going higher, higher,
rope turning and feet leaping off pavement,
history reduced to a skipping song –

> *In fourteen hundred and ninety-two*
> *Columbus sailed the ocean blue.*

In fourteen hundred and ninety-two my folk
sailed the ocean on whaling ships,
blue-eyed sailors with deft hands hauling the ropes
tacking home to feather beds over the stove
warm with the love of wives and the smell of soup,
sleeping children all around. The hearth swept,
the copper polished, the world serene. *Gezellig.*

Dutch domesticity disrupted by discovery –
not of land or water or people but of language,
the power of words, the way words could make
the kingdom of heaven here and now on earth.
Turning from Rome and King and country to be
martyred over metaphors, insisting on symbols
to the last. Then leaving familiar streets and canals
to farm Prussian valleys, Ukrainian steppes,
eventually Canadian prairies and Niagara fruitland.
A people of peace tilling the land God and King gave them,
ploughing under the Cossack turf,
planting the Indian earth,
believing their labour and love, their words,
could make the land their own.

Over the ocean blue
the people sang songs of harvest,
welcomed the strangers with their crops,
thinking earth and sky were big enough,
rivers wide enough for all to travel.

A leap of faith. The turning rope and the arched body
jumping into air, looking for thanksgiving,
hoping to land with grace in a peaceable kingdom.

V
Indian summer

Light on the water in hot October
sun in the wind after frost
boats off the bank riding gray waves
and clouds writing the autumn sky.
Traces of dead summer in Port Dalhousie –
tumbled stalks bleached with the sun
or dark with decay blaze with chrysanthemums
and scarlet yew berries, bright leaves tossing
grapes red and white on the vine.

Digging the cold wet earth,
pressing in bulbs, my fingers
find traces of other travellers.
White grub squirming, squirrel's nut,
snail coiled in its mottled shell,
fragment of blue and white china,
red brick, medicine bottle, 6-inch spike,
stones and roots and centipedes,
worms tunnelling, turning over the layers.

Uncovering the years, dis
covering what I can,
I wonder what I'd find
if I could dig deep enough,
reach far enough with my planting.
Waiting the long winter
for flowers to shake off the snow,
for red and yellow flames under the sun
and purple-black petals in the wind.

Psalms for great-grandfathers

Memorial Service 21 July 1997, Zaporozhye, Ukraine

I
Margenau: Johann Schmidt

My days are consumed like smoke
My bones are burned as an hearth
My house is taken from me and empty
I am driven from the fields of my fathers
I have eaten ashes like bread
and mingled my drink with weeping
While the children cry out with hunger
and my strong sons decline into shadows before me.

> Hans dead in Vladivostok prison:
> as the wheat failed so his life was as grass.
> Bernhard and Jakob taken:
> the wind has passed over our farms
> and the place knows them no more.
> Franz gaunt scarecrow dies in the fields,
> flesh and heart failing from famine.

Why go I mourning because of the oppression of the enemy?
O my sons who knows how close my end is?
My heart is smitten and withered like grass
So that I forget to eat my bread of ashes,
Holding a few grains of wheat in my unquiet hands.
Walking my last days with a sword in my bones
Sharp as the pain of a father who pities his children.

II
Gone to Kherson: Johann Koehn

Zagradovka. Your villages have been lifted up and cast down,
the men are gone who should work your fields.
The children are groaning, their bones cleaving to skin
and the mothers have nothing to comfort them.

> As far as the east is from the west,
> so far are my sons from me.
> David Johann Heinrich
> all gone to Kherson
> in the terror of night
> sent into Siberian exile.
> And now like pelicans of the wilderness,
> like great white owls in the desert of snow,
> their cries haunt me –
> the wings of their lives brushing death.

In Zagradovka I watch –
I am like a sparrow alone upon the house top,
Looking for a sign of their return,
Hearing their wives cry after them with mourning,
Seeing their children take tears for their meat day and night.

When I remember these things I pour out my soul in me,
For I have nothing but a few grains of wheat in my unquiet hands
and a sword in my bones all my days.
Grieving as a father for pity of my children
Here in this land of generations.

III
Sword in our bones

As a father pities his children,
So we cry out for counsel and mercy.
O may our mouths be satisfied with good things,
So that the youth of our children's children
be renewed like the eagle's
and lovingkindness live long in this land of dust;
The flowers flourish once more in the day
and in the night our hearts fill with song, –
From everlasting to everlasting
as deep calls unto deep
with the voice of joy and praise.

Sunday best

I
Sunday morning in church
      hard wooden bench
      and German droning
I sat on my father's lap
and treasured the words I could understand

     Ewigkeit. Gnade. Loben.

A world of nouns and emotion:
the rich sonorous tongue,
the full periods, the balanced phrasing,
the repetition, the delayed verb.

Like music I heard it and felt it
I tasted that sweetness
and sang with the rest

     Lobe den Herren!
     So nimm denn meine Hände.

And my father would make a raven's nest
with his callused hands and sometimes
the raven was there to grab my darting fingers
and sometimes I was safe.

And we sang

     Gott ist die Liebe

And I put my pennies in the plate.

II

Sunday afternoon
in Gramma's living room
we sat on the couch
and my father rubbed his wrist
to make pennies magically appear
out of starched cuff and sunburnt skin
while dishes moved from kitchen
to table on hushed women's voices.

       I remember the grief
of lace doilies and cyclamen and African violets,
photographs and wooden toadstools and Hummel children,
the shining silence of polished furniture
where dust was wiped each morning
when the curtains were opened
to let in the sun.

Invisible particles hanging on air
like the stories that could have been told
but were stitched instead
into pillow covers, table cloths, aprons
and the floral border on my Sunday dress.

Time out of mind

for Irene

Sometimes, a connection is made –
Brief. Sudden.
Sometimes, lives cross –
Inevitable. Unexpected.
Where were we
when we first were friends
or was it sisters?
Maybe even mother and daughter.

Was it on some crazy polder
where we plodded in *klompen*,
squeezing juice out of the earth,
thinking of red geraniums,
hanging lace in windows
and clothes on the line,
the *broekjes* flapping in wet air –
But looking always
for the flaw in the pattern,
sharing the imperfect flower,
digging in our garden at midnight
for yellow sapphires.

Or maybe in a wheatfield
crackling by a river,
far from turrets turquoise and gold
but reciting these to each other,
telling over and over the lapis lazuli,
stone upon stone in our secret horde,

while watermelons were picked,
pickles made and children fed.
Always under our kerchiefs,
quiet and correct, our brains boiled,
minds touched hidden treasures.

And this magical moment
this unlikely meeting in a strange airport
is part of all our impossible history.

You'll recognise me by my appearance
as a character in a fiction, I wrote.

And when that's not how our story turned out,
who can say the plot and characters weren't
just as I said and only the reading wrong?

You know my sister and I know your sister,
I said on the phone. *We'll know each other.*

And when the moment of recognition
didn't come, who can say who it was
we didn't know, our sisters or each other?

What craziness! we cried,
falling into each other's arms –
travellers streaming around us
intercoms calling my name.
Your face a shock to me.
Utterly unknown
and impossibly connected
with your voice over the wire.

                    But later
getting lost
and losing all direction
as we talked into the night
we accelerated out of time and space
into our story.

That car ride down the straight stretch
of the Macdonald-Cartier freeway
became our narrative.
Quite an opening!
What will happen next,
we thought, slamming the doors
of the Honda. *I have coffee,*
you said, *and apples.*
An auspicious beginning.

And then the plot development –
no exciting events
(except for wrong turns)
but lots of drawing room comedy
(you recited Sarah Binks at high speed)
with *deus ex machina*-like connections
(I told you the stranger's poems
you liked so much were actually
about a family you knew
more gossip about than I)
and even some moments of tragedy:
the lonely hero touched with death
came for awhile to sit between us
and we gave the guest silence.

Oh yes, the characterisation,
the ironies, were superb.
But was there a sense of an ending
when you drove up to the dark house
and the light spilled out
and you left me with my luggage,
the car backing slowly out,
the lights disappearing down the street
and I turned and went in the open door.
That was an end to the trip.
Maybe, I thought, *the book's closed.*
I never did like sequels.

But there's no end, no beginning, to this.
We've always been stringing beads together
with no intention of ever joining the ends.

> *When young woman meets old crone*
> *there is always food and laughter*
> *There is endless story, time out of time out of mind.*

Always wear a slip, or things my mother taught me

My mother was never a big talker
but what she said was telling.

You aren't made of pink sugar, she'd say,
You won't dissolve in a little rain.

And so I'd march off to school without an umbrella,
slogging through drizzle or downpour,
envying those who were chauffeured in the family car
and deposited, dry, at the door.

I may have been wet behind the ears
but I learned to fend for myself,
to walk with head high
through whatever the sky gods might throw at me.

Count that day lost wherein you learn nothing, she'd say.
And so I learned to take pleasure in new knowledge of any kind,
to celebrate and share the joy of finding out –
and also the fun of making it up.

How we'd laugh, sitting at the kitchen table
while I worked on a gothic paragraph for English class,
mum feeding me new words like *nefarious*
and me seizing them like a pirate's booty.

She taught me to let go to the imaginative and whimsical,
to ride the wave of an inspiration like a ship at full sail.

Mind you, she was always slim, trim, and grim,
a kind of drill sergeant manqué.
Report back to me, she'd say,
after itemising a sequence of Saturday chores.

I learned to complete my work and look around for more.
That lesson was maybe a mixed blessing.

Fashion sense, now, that's another thing she taught me.
I wouldn't wear that to a snake fight, she'd say,
Not if I knew both snakes and the referee.
And you know, I still mentally categorise certain outfits
as snake-fight suits—absolutely unwearable.

She'd set up her sewing machine on the kitchen table
and create whole wardrobes for my dolls and me.
The whirr of the machine like a cat's purr
as I played with the button box, spilling out buttons
in a kaleidoscope of colour and pattern, sorting the beauties –
a hard embossed disk of pewter,
a knobby rhinestone-studded orb,
one shaped like a strawberry from our own patch,
another stamped with a blue anchor, holding me fast at my play.

When she spent a whole day making jam or canning peaches
I'd watch her hands, swift and sure, at their work:
Washing, peeling, sorting, measuring, packing, sugaring, sealing.
Later the rows of jars in the basement fruit cellar
lined up as silent witnesses to her preservings,
a rich record written in scarlet and gold,
testifying to her care of all that had been given into her keeping.

I learned to celebrate the beauty of little things, domestic trifles.
My mother taught me to take pleasure in the moment
because a moment could be perfect, full of love and joy,
though tomorrow was uncertain and yesterday full of sorrow.

She'd tell life stories to me
when her hands were busy – when she was sewing,
or rolling out pastry, or planting bulbs.

My mother was a teacher, and she taught me life's lessons:
      to hold tightly to the things that endure
      to mark life's passages with ritual
      to listen to the heartbeats of life.

From her I learned a woman's wisdom:
      The goodness of the earth
      The endurance of generations
      The beauty of the every day
      The joy of the moment
      The love to carry on.

Pie poems

for Irma Koop Janzen

I
Flaky 1

Pies are round.
Pi r (not?) sq.
Pies are everywhere.

But
   I
      Don't
         make
           pie.
I wonder why?

Mum bakes pie.
That's why.

   I dream of apple pie –
   light flaky crust under fork
   golden juice with cinnamon scent
   fruit pieces soft and warm.

It takes a light hand
to make pastry
but any hand
can break it.

Sorry mum.
I never was good at math.

     (Wipe the cream off your face.)

II
Pie in the sky

When you stage your funeral scene
you see a host of mourners,
nervously silent. What can they say?
You lie in the casket silent as they
but with one cell still taking signals.

You sympathise with their discomfort;
It's a tense moment.
The room is suitably shrouded,
curtains hushed, flowers condoling.
Ritualised readiness and nothing
to fill this emptiness.

Throats begin to clear,
polished shoes shuffle,
downcast eyes trace patterns
on the dark carpet.
The need for an elegiac response
is overwhelming.

                        At last
the final offering is made.
From a dark corner
of the funeral parlour
a small and unknown voice
performs your final obsequies:

She made good pastry.

There is a sigh of relief.
You rest in peace.

III
Nightmare

You cut the pie in quarters, twice,
then pass around, on elegant china,
eight equitable wedges.

But something goes wrong, the pieces are returned,
you have to put them back into the pie plate,
there is an excess,
you can't make the triangles fit in the circle –

There are too many pieces.

Banana cream spills into strawberry custard,
apples peaches pears and plums ooze over the edges.
You can't mop up the drips quickly enough,
the floor is covered, you stick in syrup,
you're trapped in fruit. The kitchen becomes Pie.

You lose yourself.

IV
Apple pie

Mother cuts the apple into pieces.

Look, she says, arranging them on a plate.
Here's the mother hen. See, it's bigger than the rest.

The mother hen rocks on curved bottom,
tail feathers modestly fanned.
I can see the bright eyes in the tiny head.

And here are all the little chicks:
One, two, three, four.

The chicks nod to each other,
seek equilibrium on the edge of the plate.
One falls over.
Quickly I balance it
against the big wedge.

Go on, eat your apple pieces.

I taste death.

V
Rolling pin

I stand on a chair
to reach the counter
rolling a yellow glass marble
in my palms.
You roll the pastry.

The wooden dowel
swings back and forth,
stretching the round white dough
longer, wider, thinner –
a bedtime sheet to lift and drop
over the mound of fruit.

The rolling pin
lost its handles long ago.
There's a tunnel down the centre
I can look through like a telescope,
See you and the kitchen
through a small round window.

The hole
seems the perfect size
for my marble.
I try to
roll it
from one end
to the other.

But that yellow marble
stops
one inch down
inside the rolling pin.

For days stretching into decades
that piece of childhood play
is part of all your rolling and making.

VI
Dough

The wooden rolling pin
swings over the stretching dough.
There's no limit, your hands tell me,
to the length and width you can coax out of this pastry.
	But your voice tells another story.
A story with gaps that can't be smoothed over.

Sift measured flour, baking powder and salt into mixing bowl.

Elisabeth
on the Russian steppes, alone.
Dietrich
away with the Red Cross, in the White Army.
Snow sifting from sky
on the small black coffins
of Elise, Heinz, Woldemar:
Babies buried in the bitterness of winter.

	Death. War. Anarchy. Hunger.

Elisabeth and Dietrich
with Johann, Agnes, Victor, Henry, young Dietrich,
in the passport photo,1924.
	A fall from a horse.
	Johann does not validate his exit visa.
Louise, born April 1925, joins the exodus.

Elisabeth and Dietrich
on cold Canadian prairie
open their arms for
Irma and Ernest,
New children in the new land.

Cut in the shortening (Crisco).

Irma
in Ontario fruitland
      Your father grows stones on his farm
      turns stony hearts to flesh
      Reiseprediger. Ältester.

Irma
in the kitchen
      Your mother cuts animals
      freehand from paper,
      makes nests out of mosses and stones.

      The knives flash in the sun.

Brother Victor dies of fever, 1936.
Mother Elisabeth dies at Christmas, 1937.

Mix egg and vinegar in cup and add ice water to measured level.

Dietrich
Ice clutches his heart.
Empty arms remember.
Red leaves hang like blood from frosted limbs.
Dietrich
Marries the widow Helene October 1939,
brings home a mother to the farm.

Helene
(her cooking so good, so plentiful)
Helene
tastes vinegar.
Becomes a widow again in 1944,
loses the youngest in 1970.
Twice-widowed stepmother,
Helene's heart stops, 1974.

Add to flour and mix well.

Lorraine
in suburban kitchen. Watching.
Watching you make pie.
Listening. Listening. Listening.
These stories
Don't roll out
lie flat
fit.

These stories
I take into myself.

VII
Birth

We sit together at the kitchen table
April afternoon sunshine
spills through the window,
warms my nine-month belly.

I move in the chair
to ease the kick
rub my rib
complain
I'm tired of this.

Well
you say
> *Eat*
> *this*
> *piece*
> *of warm*
> *rhubarb*
> *pie.*
You'll have the baby by midnight.

John Adam is served up at 12:03.

Thanks mum.

VIII
Flaky 2

Single crust, double crust, lat
tice crust too!
These are the things
That you can do.

Doing and doughing
all of your days;
I'll never eat enough
to know your ways.

Roll it and pat it
and mark it with π
until the round sun
falls from the sky

and Chicken Little cries
The sky is falling! The sky is falling!

        Quick.

        Make.

        Eat.

Before the pie is opened
and the birds begin to sing.

Cross-dressing, or One is not born a woman

for Kelsey

So there you stand – naked before the mirror.
The thin wall of glass defines the space you inhabit
determines the body you fill
        The male you must be.

        You work with your hands.
Large and rough, nails thickened by concrete,
chipped by stones, palms callused
by saws and hammers.
The file rasps ragged edges,
the cotton polishes, the lotion smoothes,
delicate pink enamel transforms.

And waving slowly to dry
your hands detach themselves,
floating in the misty bathroom
like huge butterflies,
brushing, soft as kisses, your expectant face.
Making your metamorphosis,
waking Sleeping Beauty.

And then you scrape off the blond moustache,
emblem of your manhood for 15 years,
your upper lip tender, exposed, vulnerable –
a quivering line saying *this is me is me*,
after so many years of asking *where* and *what*
and not hearing any answers.

But it isn't enough.
You add paint and powder,
make blue eyes bluer, lashes darker,
cheeks round and pink, curving lips outlined,
and finally, a teased blond mane of hair.

You take a walk on the wild side.

Now the mirror looks back at you with the face
of the daughter your mother never had;
the girl you wanted to be;
the woman you will yourself to be.
But still your body of hair and muscle and beef
mocks your face, declares the mask.

A false front is needed.

The basic black dress, the pearls,
the control top pantyhose, the special size 12 heels
bought at a theatrical supply shop,
complete the transformation. You become *the other* –
the other in yourself, the woman you had to deny.

And I listen and listen to your story, my dinner getting
cold and I hold the photograph of your most recent masquerade
and I imagine all of this and I imagine all the past between us, the
unimaginable past of blood and history and stories told and stories
not told and here is a new story at last, a new narrative, a plot I've
never entered. And I hear you say cross-dressing puts you in
touch with women, teaches you respect for their lives and I listen
to your story about how you almost ploughed a guy in a bar for
pinching your ass in its short tight skirt.

And I hear you say cross-dressing gets you in touch with your feminine side. *The feminine.* The love, the tenderness, the sensitivity, the life of the emotions. And I don't even counter with the anti-essentialist argument because I hear you say cross-dressing makes you whole, that for 30 years you were miserable, you couldn't live the script you'd been given, you were oppressed by male myths. The big construction worker, the business man, the achiever, the strong silent one. The boss.

And I think about your courage, your refusal to live the plots of gender and class, your middle-age rebirth –
And I think maybe you are a woman, after all.

All this, dear coz, is just to tell you
when I look in my mirror
I see a female impersonator too.

Alice poems

I
Alison Wonderland

for Alison

Circling
    and
       circling
          I circle
back
to the stage we first played together
making shadows on the walls
singing stories in rhythms
without words.
We were dancers in a *pas de deux*,
unable to tell where one body flowed into the other.

      Encircling you,
carrying your body
light
as my own breath,
I feel you
moving away from me
into the spotlight.

And dangerously
deliberating possession
I delay your solo entry,
hold you
in our arabesque
for one timeless moment
before letting you dance
alone.

Watching in the green room
twisting the cloth in my hands
I see your slow and secret smile,
your eyes inviting me
to support you again
in your jumps and twists
and breathless momentary poses.

And watching you spin away –
leap, with all your sunlit energy
and return, soft as the catch
of my breath –
I try not to fear gravity too much;
the hurt your beautiful body
might feel here
in this shifting space
of uncertain footing.

And think instead
how you move full of grace,
my Tuesday's child, full of wonder.
Believing the story's name
is Alison Wonderland.

II
White knight

John G. Janzen 1923-2003

Old man
Old man with white whiskers
and love in your eyes
I think about all those years
stretching behind us,
a road going back to your boyhood
under prairie skies in Delorraine –
that swath of sod you cut from the earth
in naming me,
so I could carry a piece of the land
that fed you all the days of my life.

We shared the land, the sky.
Your eyes clear and blue
as you rode along telling stories,
me listening, walking beside you –
a hand, sometimes, on the saddle
hung round with the claptrap
of possibilities,
        achievements,
             failures.
And I asked about some of these,
examined the intricate handmade gear;
but so many – most – are strange museum pieces
bearing no legends, or secret containers
hidden under the saddle blanket.

And as you rode beside me
(always with the reins loose in your hands)
when I saw the horse's unsteady gait,
your headlong tumbles,
I just kept talking and listening,
pretending with you
nothing had happened.

And now that the road
is narrowing, the ditches
getting deeper all the time,
I need to tell you, old man,
what we both already know.
I need to say
if I didn't help you up
all those times I walked beside you
it was because I loved
your humour
your buoyancy
your eagerness for more adventures
and the way you always
carried life full
in your open hands.

III
Alice underground

Alice Vandermolen Kooistra 1926-1992

No rain falls underground.
No stars shine or icy branches knock.
Flowers are painted there,
speaking in unnatural, unheard of voices.

Buried worlds speak to the living,
turning over dark passages,
opening sudden pits under running feet
until one tiny self survives,
swimming in a sea of oceanic tears
shed by another, a giant, self.

This is why we eat cake
at birthdays, weddings, funerals;
each swallowed crumb saying
>   *you are little, you are big,*
>   *you are going or gone.*

The taste of dying years
sticking to the throat, blurring the clear,
the impassioned, inarticulate cry.

Graveyard tunes

Hi ma –
just thought I'd call;
haven't talked in awhile.
Wanted to let you know –

    that Saturday before you died?

– I was playing hooky from days of dying,
thinking maybe if I drove far enough into alien landscape
I wouldn't see Death at every corner, thumbing a ride.

I know. Never pick up a stranger. But ma, I knew this guy,
or thought I did. What do you ever really know, anyway? –
A name, a face, a gesture, an implied history, maybe.
Like a half-remembered melody you find yourself hum
ming, a reverberating chord. Enharmonic echo.

So I picked him up en route to nowhere.
He had his own voice to haunt him,
eyes to compel him, death to discover or deny.

We travelled together the length of a March afternoon.
Your last Saturday.
What did the ceiling, the walls, look like?
After so much living, so much life,

A silent room. A narrow bed. A closed window.

Where did we go? You'll never believe it, ma.
I played hooky from death
by wandering through a graveyard.

Sleet drumming us with icy fingers,
headstones lined up like black keys.
Two strangers looking for a stranger's grave
among rows of death indiscriminate.
A hundred years and more of dying
under the spruce trees.

He coughing and wrapped in a muffler,
me blowing my nose, losing my hat,
wishing for warmth and wisdom –
A manual. A guide. A mother.

We make our way to the place.
The wind a knife through the heart.
Snow on the flat stone:
stark letters, graven date,
etched keyboard. Middle C.

> *So little to sum up a life*, Pat said.
> *So little*, I thought, *to mark a death*.

Are you laughing ma?
The Band's too loud, I can't hear you.

Ghost

for P.F.

You have ghosts all around you
Norah of the North said that time
she couldn't read my pain.
Now I've met one of them in the flesh.

This ghost drinks Cuban beer,
eats black beans and corn tortillas
at the Havana in East Vancouver
Jaywalks in sandals
with purple painted toes.

A nomad of no place and no time
moving through Europe and Portage at Main,
St. Mary riding with him to the next stop.
Train whistles blowing in the long empty night.

He carries the North Sea with him
to creeks where time stops
to whaling ships moored on the prairies
to this city of mountains and mainliners.
Songs of many lands in his veins.

I felt the words bleed through his skin
when I bandaged his wound,
blond hair on his arm under my fingertips
electric with the sound of guitars
playing all night in Winnipeg bars.

Long ago, so long ago.
The sea is vast, the prairies endless,
mountains fill the sky.

There's no place for my ghost to go
but this all too certain flesh,
this stop on the way to the stars.

Preservings

There's a ghost
in my mother's typewriter.

It eats the endings of her words.

She's noticed for awhile now
how the last letter of a word
goes missing, drops off
into blank space.

Soon, she thinks, the
next-to-last letter will be gone
and then the one before that
and the one before that
and so on, until there are
no words left.

      Nothing but a white sheet.

As a child she'd taken to heart
her old aunt's warning
that she'd be held accountable
on the Judgement Day
for every unnecessary word.

She took to storing them up,
preserving especially the past,
story upon story sealed in jars
and arranged neatly on rows
of newspaper-lined shelves
in the cold room –

      Ready for opening.

Only on special days
did I taste the firm golden peaches,
pale pears, sour cucumbers,
pickled beets, sweet strawberry jams.

She was a careful woman,
knowing that to each of us
a certain allotment was given at birth.

When we've used up all our words
our time on earth is up, she said.

And so she thought of
all those lost letters
dropping from her keyboard
and missing the page
as signs of her mortality,
warnings that her little preserve
of words was near its end.

With so little time left
I wish she'd open her hoardings,
share to the last syllable
the sweet and the bitter,
give me enough words
to understand.

Dead woman talking

Pay attention!
the corpse hissed
This is important –

      Vital.

It's tough having a cadaver in your office.
The body takes up so much space
it's hard to work around it
without tripping on an arm or a leg.
It's a stiff.

She's sitting in my chair
leaning on my desk
naked as the day she was born.
Not a pretty sight.

After awhile the papers under her arms
start to get slimy
I can't retrieve lost articles
memos become illegible
even the computer keys get sticky.

I try to take care of her properly,
clip her nails, brush her hair,
say *excuse me* if I bump into her;
move her around in my big swivel chair
let her look out the window sometimes
introduce her to colleagues.

None of this does any good.
She just keeps telling me to *pay attention*.
She's really raising a big stink about this;
it's like she's fixated or something –
like she can't let go.

I wish she'd just chill out.

        Once I lost my temper
told her to drop dead.

That's when she got really dangerous.

        Nowadays we hang together a lot
neither of us doing anything much.
I'm learning how to spell time
it's a matter of life or death.

Dead secret

There are problems resuscitating a corpse.
      Resistance, for example.
      Maybe he wants to stay in the place he has gone.

And who am I, anyway,
thinking I can breathe life into an empty sack
inflate a collapsed heart
staunch a perpetual wound
pull a dead body up from underground.

Some things are better left buried.

Light a candle and leave.

Harbouring angels unawares

You never know when you might meet an angel.

They like rainy days best;
Maybe it makes travelling easier for them.

They try to find you alone
At a point of transition or transit.
In a metro station maybe or an airport taxi.

They seek you out in foreign lands
As if they know that's when you're
most vulnerable to strangers,
most likely to find personal intrusion forgivable.

It's funny about angels.
They always give the same message in different forms,
a series of post cards from faraway places
picturing scenes of incredible beauty
and architectural splendour.

> *Having a wonderful time,*
> *Wish you were here.*

Singing the sacred

Without words nothing would be sacred.

This shard of bone or scrap of cloth,
this piece of land, drop of water, lighted candle

     is only bone, cloth, earth, water, fire.

Without the breath of story
to inspire them
there would be no spirits
stirring us with their presence.

We would not build glass cases to house them,
fashion, with infinite patience,
filigree of gold to reveal and conceal
this silent matter
or build monuments of stone to mark their place,
etch plaques of brass in their honour,
travel by car or boat or foot or wrinkled knee
the distance to their dwellings.

Year after year after year
generation upon generation
word by word we build worlds
the sacred can inhabit.

We want to go to a space outside time,
to experience a moment larger than life,
an imagined paradise
where the saints watch and wait
while we weave webs of words
to make the silent speak.

In our human way
wanting the warm body of language
to wrap our shivering mortalities in
so our bare and unclothed selves
can touch and feel and take fire.

Wise woman's garden

for Martha

In a garden edged with fir trees
ablaze with flowers from bud to blossom
tangled with stalks and leaves
and the layers of growth and decay
there's a tall straight woman
who walks with the Old Ones.

She has magic in her bones;
she chants ancient spells
over bole and bloom
rock and root,
celebrating the phases of the moon
as season changes to season
and the earth turns over again.

She makes stone paths
And water gardens in barrels;
she trains vines on trellises
and cultivates herbs.

She knows that every garden
needs a guardian spirit;
hers is a bronze Cupid,
shocking the hollyhocks and stargazer lilies
piercing the fairy roses and black-eyed Susan's
with arrows of love,
making this sandy soil sacred to summer joy.

Giving the wise woman
a piece of growing green
to carry in her sage heart
through long nights of rue
and white winter days of silence and slow thyme.

Naming poem for a naming day

for Martha and Murat
in honour of F.E.A.T.

Crowned with the moon
the stars sing, the forest wakes,
the universe enters your small white house,
brings food to your table, saying
> *In the last days of Ramadan*
> *After the long fast*
> *Now is the time to feast.*

I touch this miracle of winter
with gentle fingers, feeling the warmth
of the small perfect body.
The world is not big enough
to hold this joy, this promise.

A gift of Maytime seeding
blossoming in frozen January
when glacial gardens guard memories
of hollyhock seeds and stargazer lilies
sleeping under blankets of snow.

Lullabied by the moon
a universe of love touches
the deep forest of dreams,
brings a small warm son
to your white winter home,
filling your empty arms.

Martindale Pond

At twilight I lace on my skates,
glide off the edge of the world.

unreal landscape

Ice pulling down the sky
a lover looking to lose herself
under white weight,
to find the melting point,
ground zero of flesh
or maybe spirit.
The ease of forgetfulness.

The air is haunted by grey voices.
Unseen on the other side
a flock of Canada geese
huddle against bank and bush,
black throats raised to the lowering sky,
calling and calling.
The sound beating round me
in winged flurries.

The grief of memory's echo:
a single oak leaf
trapped in ice
and the cut of my blades
on the snow-flecked surface.

Winter rain

I

There's a hole in my heart
where you passed through

A tunnel of ice
bored by winter rain.

II

Outside my window
there's a snow woman in the garden
almost my size
though not my shape.

The snow woman's smile
is carved so deep
it will take days
of this November sleet
to turn its face to tears.

At night the snow woman
pirouettes in place,
lifting white skirts
above the wet earth.

In the morning
she's so still
I think
she's a dead woman.

III

There's a hole in my heart
where you passed through

I've kept the bullet
wrapped in burlap.

In the spring
I'll plant it in my garden.